QUAYLE
HUNTING

Carroll & Graf Publishers, Inc.
New York

QUAYLE HUNTING

THE DAN QUAYLE JOKE BOOK

Bill Adler & Bill Adler, Jr.

First Carroll & Graf edition 1992

Carroll & Graf Publishers, Inc.
260 Fifth Avenue
New York, NY 10001

ISBN: 0-88184-825-5

Book design by Oksana Kushnir

Manufactured in the United States of America

To the East College Gang: Mitch, Bill, and Brett.

ACKNOWLEDGMENTS

Plenty of people contributed their humor to this collection. While the responsibility for any jokes that fall flat on their face must rest with us, we would like to take this opportunity to thank those who have served in the cause of humor: Peggy Robin, Beth Pratt-Dewey, Paul Harris, host of "Harris in the Morning" on WTEM, Washington, DC, Marc Perkel, Deborah Werfman, Elaina Newport, Jack Curtain, Judy Russell, Daniel Capano, Bob Smart and, of course, Dan Quayle.

CONTENTS

INTRODUCTION

My country has, in its wisdom,
contrived for me the most insignificant
office [the vice-presidency] that
ever the invention of man contrived
or his imagination conceived.

John Adams
in a letter to Abigail Adams,
December 19, 1789

What a fun book to write! We really mean it. Most of the time authors struggle against deadlines; with the *Dan Quayle Joke Book* we never wanted the research to end. They say that living through a time of great technological change—such as the invention of the telephone, personal computer, or smokeless ash tray—can give you an exciting lifetime. Well, there's even more fun in the universe: Watching Dan Quayle. Honestly, we haven't had such a good time since Spiro Agnew.

Don't feel sorry for Dan Quayle because of all the fun that's being made of him. Humor has immortalized the man. Unless you're a contender on "Jeopardy," you probably don't know more than a dozen vice-presidents: But you'll probably be telling Dan Quayle jokes forever.

Well, we don't want to take up too much of your time. Go ahead—read this book and enjoy.

Q·U·A·Y·L·E

HUNTING

By Jeff MacNelly. Copyright 1988. Reprinted by permission: Tribune Media Services.

DAN JUST DOING HIS JOB

How can the Vice-President's assistant tell when he has been using the computer?
There is White Out on the monitor!

•

Dan Quayle was inducted into the Little League Hall of Fame today. The flattered Vice-President said he was honored, but this would be his last year as a player.

•

The President called Dan into the Oval Office and said, "I want to do something that will show the nation I have faith in you, your maturity and sense of responsibility . . . Would you like a puppy?"

•

Who keeps changing the bulbs for the thousand points of light?
Hey, that's what George hired Dan for.
Well, that explains it then.
So that's why they're a thousand dim bulbs!

How does Dan Quayle define Roe v. Wade?
Two ways to cross the Potomac.

•

*What is 15 inches long and hangs down directly in front of a
horse's ass?*
Dan Quayle's necktie.

•

Have you heard that Quayle is getting a 25% pay raise?
And why not? The White House lawn has been looking
pretty damn good lately.

•

What's the difference between a hawk and a Quayle? None.

•

Quayle went to the bathroom. Got a load off his mind.

This summer, Vice-President Quayle is expected to star in a new TV series called "America's LEAST Wanted."

●

If Dan Quayle were his wife, he'd be pointing at dinette sets on game shows.

●

The North American bird with the tiniest brain and biggest ambition is the Quail.

●

Dan Quayle was at Tampa Stadium for an important football game. He was there to throw out the first drunk.

●

What do you get when you cross a chicken with a hawk?
A Quayle.

When the Bush administration took office, there was a high official who took as his chief foreign policy adviser a man who in 1984 had published an English-language translation of Aristotle's Politics. *That broad-minded official was:*
(a) James Baker
(b) Dick Darman
(c) George Bush
(d) Dick Cheney
(e) Dan Quayle.
Answer: (e) Dan Quayle

•

More than one person has remarked "Dan, You're No Strunk and White."

•

Dan Quayle—looks great: Less filling—99% content free.

•

Dan Quayle is the Veepette.

To demonstrate that Quayle was more of an ordinary guy than a member of the elite, the White House arranged to have Quayle filmed taking out his garbage, putting it on his curb.
Guess he was practicing his duties as Vice-President.

•

The Vice-President is such a find that the comics have voted him their Most Valuable Politician.

•

How is Dan Quayle like a teenager?
He always wants to borrow the keys to the ship of state.

•

Newspaper headline July 9, 1991:
QUAYLE SAYS COURT NOMINEE THOMAS NEED NOT DISCLOSE VIEW ON CONSTITUTION
Newspaper headline July 10, 1991:
QUAYLE SAYS COURT NOMINEE THOMAS NEED NOT DISCLOSE HE IS BLACK

Dan Quayle: The Thing Without A Brain.

•

Another way of looking at Quayle is as term insurance.

•

Quayle has inspired the notion that the vice-presidency should be a means for supplying spare parts for American political leadership.

•

When asked whether he's worried that Bush will drop him from the 1992 ticket, Quayle responds, "No, I'm not worried —I have the photographs."

•

A lot of people feel Quayle is just too inexperienced for a do-nothing job, like the vice-presidency.

Looking into Dan Quayle's radiant blue eyes is like looking out the window.

●

George Bush often treats Dan Quayle as a little puppy, a lap dog. "Gee, Barbara, can I keep him?" the President asked his wife. "Okay, George, but you'll have to feed him and take care of him and get him his shots. He'll be your responsibility." "Oh, I will, I will, I promise," the male Bush replied. "And what are you going to call him, George?" "Uh . . . the Vice-President of the United States." "That's nice, George. Now make sure he goes on the paper."

●

It's no surprise why Marilyn Quayle selected federal disaster relief as her favorite charity.

●

When George Bush said that Quayle would definitely be on the ticket in 1992, America's comedians said, **"Thank you!"**

By Jim Borgman. Copyright 1990. Reprinted by permission: King Features Syndicate, Inc.

The Secret Service has been instructed to shoot John Sununu, James Baker, or anyone else with a bulging attaché case who tries to force his way in with intent to brief Dan Quayle on the issues.

•

Why is Dan Quayle qualified to head the National Space Council? He took up space in school.

•

After the meeting . . .
Later, while being interviewed by a reporter, Thatcher apparently forgot about her meeting with Quayle. When reminded, she responded that indeed she had met with Quayle for half an hour, but that it had slipped her mind.

•

The new Haitian president, aware of his predecessor's assassination, had taken "extraordinary steps to ensure his safety"—making Quayle his Vice-President.

Why did former Prime Minister Margaret Thatcher enjoy meeting Dan Quayle?
She took great pleasure in meeting someone lower in the polls than herself.

•

Did you hear about Dan Quayle's new book? He just finished coloring the last page.

•

Dan Quayle has helped the English language by neutering the word "bimbo."

•

Have you heard of the Dan Quayle savings bond? It has no interest and no maturity.

•

Dan Quayle has been called "an impressive deficit."

•

George Bush and Dan Quayle are fishing. An aide rushes over with a list of twenty foreign crises that they ought to get excited about. They look at him and keep fishing.

•

Dan Quayle always said he would have scored much higher on his SAT's if the guy in the seat next to him had studied harder.

•

"DAD, THEY'RE CALLING UP THE RESERVES!"

By Paul Conrad. Copyright 1990, Los Angeles Times. Reprinted with permission.

DAN AT WAR

*What will be the name of the film focusing on the wartime exploits
of Vice-President Dan Quayle?*
It will be called *Full Dinner Jacket.*

•

President Bush was in Canada over the weekend. He asked
Dan Quayle to go with him, but Quayle said, "I don't
have to go because my dad can get me into the
National Guard."

•

*There is a new sandwich in a Washington, DC, restaurant
named after Quayle.*
It is half chicken and half turkey.

•

Dan Quayle's family fortune is said to be worth some $200
million. People were shocked that a guy with $200 million
didn't go to Vietnam. The only guy with that much
money who went to Vietnam was Bob Hope.

You can pick on Dan all you want, but don't knock the National Guard. It's not their fault he joined them.

•

What do you get when you cross a chicken with a hawk?
A Vice-President who calls for war in the Middle East, but spent his own draft years in the National Guard.

•

If the Viet Cong attacked Muncie, Dan Quayle was ready.

•

The *Indianapolis 500* was the name of Quayle's old Army combat outfit.

•

What is a Quayle?
A bird that ducks.

Johnny Carson once described his in-studio audience as "the kind of group that would buy Dan Quayle a tape of *Good Morning, Vietnam.*"

●

Then there's the story of Dan Quayle swapping war stories with Pat Robertson, another would-be war hero who used family influence to avoid combat.

●

Dan Quayle served much of his military career in his home state. Perhaps one day they'll make a movie out of it: *Thirty Seconds Over Indianapolis.*

●

How vital was Dan's role in the National Guard during the Vietnam War? This joke reveals the answer:
How many National Guardsmen does it take to screw in a light bulb? A hundred. One to put in the light bulb and the rest to keep an eye out for the Viet Cong.

Not one square foot of Indiana fell to the Viet Cong when Dan Quayle was in the National Guard.

•

Why did the chicken cross the road?
To join the National Guard.

•

Why didn't Quayle go to Canada to avoid the war?
He wasn't sure where it was.

•

When we went to war with Iraq, Danny had to call his dad again.

•

While the National Guard is no longer a joke, Dan Quayle still is.

One of Dan Quayle's responsibilities in the National Guard was to make cool explosion sounds when the platoon trained with dummy grenades.

●

The President called up the National Guard and the Army Reserve, and we didn't see Quayle for a month.

●

What's the difference between Dan Quayle and Jane Fonda?
Jane Fonda went to Vietnam.

●

On the Vice-President's trip to Panama:
First we invade them, then we send Quayle. Talk about a one-two punch.

●

Not long after Iraq invaded Kuwait, the Vice-President was in Jacksonville, Florida. A local radio station announced that he was there to check on the crisis in the Gulf.

●

While Quayle didn't serve in Vietnam, he saw the movie *Platoon* five times and that "was good enough for me."

●

If Quayle were cast in a Vietnam movie, he'd have a nonspeaking part.

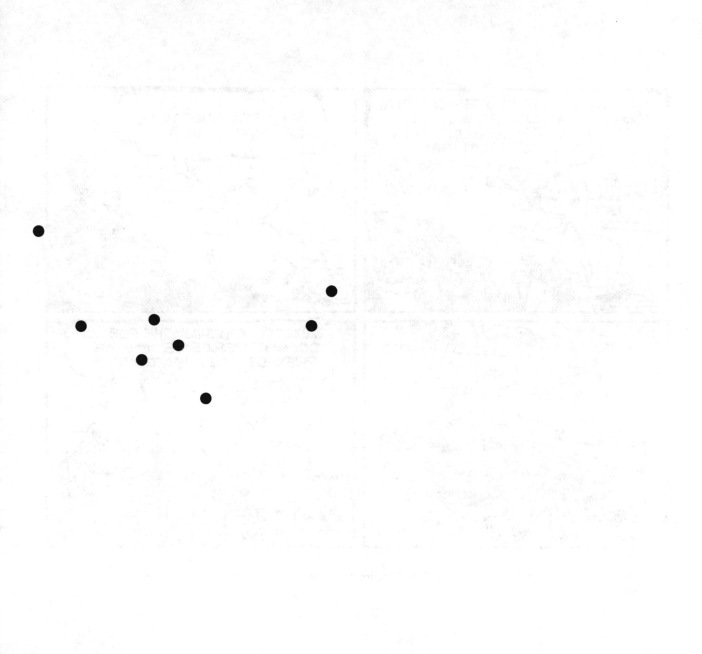

By Chuck Asay. Copyright 1991. Reprinted with permission: Chuck Asay of the Colorado Springs Gazette Telegraph.

QUAYLE
AS PRESIDENT

In the event that Quayle assumes the presidency, the following might occur at his swearing in:
Supreme Court Justice: "President Quayle, raise your right hand."
Supreme Court Justice: "The other right hand."

•

What's the good news about Vice-President Dan Quayle's getting a 25% pay raise?
Better that than a promotion.

•

While J. Danforth Quayle well deserves to inherit the family silver tea service, he's not fit to inherit Bush's new world order.

•

Many Americans think that Dan Quayle's purpose is to provide jokes for Jay Leno, David Letterman, and Arsenio Hall and, frankly, many Americans would sleep better believing that to be true.

Dan Quayle is the only American who has consistently striven to attain the number-two position.

•

If Quayle becomes President, the Secret Service won't have to take its job seriously.

•

Here's the advantage of a Quayle presidency: Americans can watch him grow up on TV.

•

Dan Quayle is considered a hot TV guest because he might screw up.

•

Why should Quayle be President?
He has personally spoken to the leaders of many other countries.

Even the most ardent Quayle supporters have to admit that Dan Quayle is the butt of plenty of jokes. And there's no way that the President of the United States is unaware of these jokes. Once when asked "How do you feel about the possibility of Dan Quayle taking over the presidency?" Bush replied, "Only over my dead body."

•

What does Quayle have going for him as a possible President? He's in such good health that he'll be able to serve two terms without anything happening.

•

By Walt Handelsman. Copyright 1991. Reprinted by permission: Tribune Media Services.

DON'T FEEL
SORRY FOR DAN

"He looks like a little boy who just wet his pants," says Elaine Bole, editor of *Capitol Comedy*, a newsletter of quips used by politicians all over Washington. She was explaining how his insecurities and uptight ways make him an easy comedy target.

•

Dan Quayle's so slow, it takes him two hours to watch "Sixty Minutes."

•

Dan is as:
dumb as a box of rocks
smart as algae
stupid as mud.

•

Word has it that Dan Quayle was on a secret buying mission for the National Endowment for the Arts when he acquired the well-endowed Chilean doll.

Why did Dan take his wife and 16 of his closest friends to the movies the other day?
He had seen a sign there saying "Under 17 not admitted."

•

President Bush visited a Virginia high school the other day. He spoke to the students about the importance of education, giving one dramatic example: "If you study hard and get good grades, you can grow up to be President. But if you don't study, well, Dan, would you come out here, please?"

•

What were the three hardest years of Dan Quayle's life?
The second grade.

•

The Quayle-for-President campaign is developing its themes. Through a national polling service they're trying out this one: Quayle's average intelligence makes it possible for him to relate to most Americans.

Dan Quayle is actually very respectful when he sits behind George Bush. Not once during President Bush's State of the Union address did Quayle make rabbit ears behind his head.

●

Here's what they say about the Bush administration:
That's 999 points of light and 1 dim bulb.

●

Dan Quayle's problem is that he's 5′ 9″, but the water is 6 feet deep.

●

Good thing for Quayle it's not possible to flunk the job of Vice-President.

●

Dan Quayle is a man gifted with a unique set of disabilities.

In 1980 Quayle took a golfing trip to Florida with a group of politicians including the famous lobbyist, Paula Parkinson, who later alleged that Quayle made a pass at her. Quayle denied it. Quayle's wife, Marilyn, supported Dan, saying, "Anyone who knows Dan Quayle knows that given a choice between golf and sex, he'd choose golf every time."

•

To decrease the national debt, the Treasury Department will soon begin offering the Dan Quayle savings bond. The only trouble is it takes about 43 years to mature.

•

On television Quayle sounds like a scared kid trying desperately to remember lines some adult made him memorize.

•

Quayle has been called The Dummy Laureate of the United States.

The answer is "Indianapolis 500." What is the question? The question is: Where did Dan Quayle take his SAT's and what was the total score.

●

What do you get Dan Quayle for his birthday?
A Mickey Mouse watch.

Does this mean that Mickey Mouse got a Dan Quayle watch?

●

Quayle returned home to Indiana for summer camp with his 10-year-old daughter. Just because he's Vice-President, doesn't mean he has to change good family habits. His daughter kissed her daddy on the cheek, and said she'd be back in a month to pick him up.

●

Dan Quayle writes his own material, so comedians have nothing to worry about.

Dan was thrilled when David Letterman invited him to appear on his late-night show. However, he declined the invitation with regret when he learned Letterman wanted him to perform in the "Stupid Pet Tricks" segment of the show.

•

When Barbara Bush launched full force ahead with her illiteracy campaign, she started with the toughest project first: Dan Quayle.

•

During the campaign, George Bush reiterated his "thousand points of light" theme. What he didn't explain, however, was that it cast a shadow over Dan Quayle's head.

•

Everyone's heard the story of the anatomically correct doll that Dan Quayle purchased. What's less known, however, is that Quayle was spotted attending a collector's convention to replace the doll that Jesse Helms confiscated.

Found in a classified advertisement in *The Washington Times:*
MISSING: One Donald Duck Wallet. If found call
Vice-President Dan Quayle.

●

It has been reported that Marilyn Quayle was upset that
reporters, who often chide her for having even less of a career
than her husband, wrote that she was planning to start
a new career writing fiction. Marilyn insisted she had
plenty of experience preparing Dan's resume.

●

What Dan Quayle should call his autobiography: *How to
Succeed in Politics Without Really Trying.*

●

A Quaylism:
Some people are born into greatness.
Some people have it thrust upon them.
And some people receive it as a graduation present.

Why did Dan Quayle get so many parking tickets at college?
He stopped putting money in the meter when gumballs
didn't come out.

•

Quayle has been accused of using connections to get into law
school in a program designed for the disadvantaged. How do
we know this? When Quayle addressed the question on the
application, "Do you have a handicap?" he wrote, "Yes,
two strokes."

•

When Quayle hijacked an airplane he demanded two dollars
and 500,000 parachutes.

•

Quayle has his fans:
Joke writers.

"...I KNEW SPIRO AGNEW... SPIRO AGNEW WAS A FRIEND OF MINE... AND VICE-PRESIDENT QUAYLE... YOU'RE NO SPIRO AGNEW..."

By Bill Schorr. Copyright 1988. Reprinted by permission: UFS, Inc.

LAWYERS' JOKES

By Dana Summers. Copyright 1991, Washington Post Writers Group. Reprinted with permission.

DAN QUAYLE TRIVIA QUIZ

(Thanks to Paul Harris, host of "Harris in the Morning" on WTEM in Washington, DC)

In 1989, at a party for his 42nd birthday, what did the Vice-President do when asked to make a wish before blowing out the candles on his birthday cake?
a) Shake his head, saying, "I can't think of any"
b) **Growl and point a knife at the throat of PBS reporter Judy Woodruff**
c) Suck helium out of a balloon, and imitate a munchkin from *The Wizard of Oz* singing Happy Birthday

•

When he first meets a man, Quayle has a habit of doing what?
a) Giving the man a high-five
b) Repeating the man's name six times to memorize it
c) **Shaking the man's hand vigorously and punching him in the arm**

•

Which of these is Dan Quayle's favorite movie?
a) *Hoosiers*
b) *Caddyshack*
c) ** *Ferris Bueller's Day Off* **

In an NBC television interview shortly after the presidential election, how did Dan Quayle describe himself?
a) **A huge question mark**
b) Older than a lot of people my age
c) Presidential lumber

•

How did Marilyn Quayle describe her husband?
a) A sex machine
b) **A studious sort**
c) A great Hoosier

•

How did the Vice-President address a group of Samoans when he visited American Samoa?
a) How . . . me represent great white chief in Washington
b) **You all look like happy campers to me**
c) Aloha . . . surf's up!

•

What were the Vice-President's first words when he called Secretary of Transportation Samuel Skinner to invite him to the Indianapolis 500?
a) Hello, this is Mario Andretti. Is Al Unser there?
b) **Vrrroooom, vrrrroooom, vrrrroooom!**
c) Hey, Sammy baby, how about seeing some real transportation?

•

During the vice-presidential debate, what did Quayle say he would do if he unexpectedly became President?
a) Call Marilyn and ask her what to do next
b) **Say a prayer and call a cabinet meeting**
c) Go on national television and tell the American people that their worst fears had been realized

•

In 1976, when asked by an Indiana GOP county chairman to run for Congress, what was Quayle's response?
a) Congress is for sissies
b) What are the golf courses like down there?
c) **I'll have to check with my dad**

During the 1988 campaign, what commercial slogan did Quayle use to describe the head of the ticket?

a) **"The heartbeat of America**

b) The quicker picker upper

c) Everything you always wanted in a President, and less.

●

How did Marilyn Quayle describe her role during Dan's first congressional campaign?

a) I gave him a brown bag lunch every day, always with a Twinkie in it

b) **I made all the decisions**

c) I wouldn't let him watch "Hogan's Heroes"

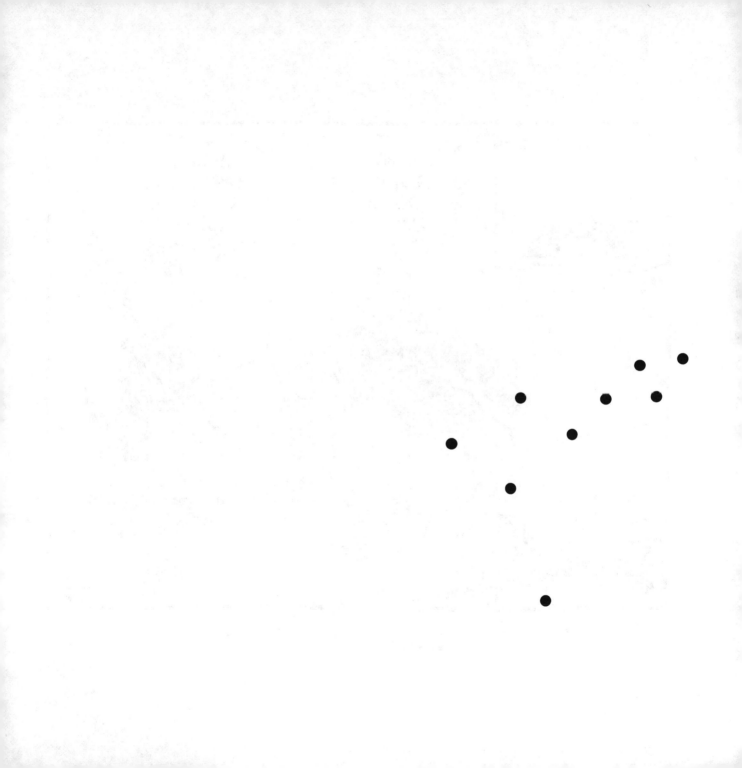

By Dan Wasserman. Copyright 1991, Boston Globe. Distributed by the Los Angeles Times Syndicate. Reprinted with permission.

DAN'S
GEOGRAPHY

Dan Quayle needs a little education about foreign affairs. He thought Shamir was the name of a killer whale.

•

Quayle tried to explain on CBS's "Face the Nation" just what was going on with the Kurds just after the end of the Gulf War. "Let me try to put it in perspective for you . . . The northern part of the country, more unstable than the southern part, was almost total chaos even though Hussein controlled Baghdad. A couple of the holy cities, there's some serious problems. But on the whole, yes, there is instability, there is insurrection, and this is not to be totally unexpected."

•

Why does Dan think he's the perfect man to handle Middle Eastern issues? "Because I'm from the Middle West," he says.

•

On the 20th anniversary of man walking on the moon, Quayle sent Michael Jackson a telegram.

Says Quayle, "I love California. I grew up in Phoenix." (He really said this!)

•

Why is Dan Quayle in favor of the Stealth bomber?
He thinks it looks like Batman's plane.

•

Right after the San Francisco earthquake President Bush calls Quayle into his office and tells him, "Dan, I need firsthand information. I'd like you to visit the epicenter."
Quayle says, "Hey, neat, Mr. President! And while I'm there, do you mind if I pop over to Disney World, too?"

•

The Vice-President left on a trip to Central America today, and said on departure he was looking forward to seeing Central America again, "especially Ohio, Indiana, and Nebraska."

Dan Quayle always said that Red China should be served on a white tablecloth.

•

Dan Quayle is reported to have said that he used to be a Batman fan until he took the job as number 2.

•

Dan Quayle thinks that Ukraine is a sex organ.

"DO YOU, GEORGE BUSH, PROMISE TO PRESERVE, PROTECT AND DEFEND THE CONSTITUTION...
AND SWEAR YOU WON'T DIE, SO HELP YOU GOD?!"

WHEN GEORGE
GOT SICK

Who's the second most important man in the Bush administration?
His doctor.

•

When Bush had a brief heart "error," T-shirts appeared saying, "President's Prayer Club" on the front and "Keep George Healthy" on the back.

•

The Secret Service has orders that if George Bush is shot, they're to shoot Quayle.

•

Someone pointed out that the term "Dan Quayle joke" is redundant.

•

Remember: Vice-President Quayle is only a deadbeat away.

One patriotic American says:
Although I support the war effort in the Middle East and by
extension the President, I must admit I did not vote for him.
Nevertheless, once he was elected, I found religion . . .
Every night I get down on my knees and pray fervently . . .
For the life of George Bush!

•

When George Bush was sick Quayle was standing by—to be
a heart donor.

•

When President George Bush took ill, the whole world lived
in terror that something might happen to George. How's that
for life insurance?

•

With the possibility of George Bush being incapacitated, Dan
Quayle telephoned Ronald Reagan. He wanted to know what
it's like to be an acting President.

A nightmare or fairytale—you pick:

One day George Bush takes ill and goes into a coma for two years, thus making Dan President. When George comes out of the coma he is very concerned about how Dan has been running the country the past two years, so he asks to see him. When Dan deigns to see him, George says, "Well, Dan, you've had your hand at the helm for two years now, so I'd like to ask you a few questions about how things are going. Such as what is the current rate of inflation?" Dan says, "It's down to 2.5% and we expect it to keep coming down and level off at 1%." George is quite surprised and asks, "Well, what's the unemployment rate?" Dan answers, "2%, just about everybody in the country has a good job." George is very impressed but still a little doubtful, so he asks, "How large is the national debt?" Dan responds, "We no longer have a national debt, it's been paid off." George, now awed, says, "You know, Dan, I have to admit that I was quite worried about how you would run the country, but you seem to have done a magnificent job, I'm really impressed. Oh, by the way, just out of curiosity, how much does a loaf of bread cost?" Dan answers, "Oh, around a hundred yen."

•

There was a near emergency: Quayle dialed 811.

Dan kept telling everyone, "Buy American! Buy American!" Obviously, the Japanese were listening.

•

What are the most feared words in the Republican Party? "Dan, I'm not feeling very well."

•

Bush, Quayle and New York's Governor Mario Cuomo were on a helicopter flying over the Bronx to determine if federal money should be used for improvement. Cuomo said, "I'm going to make 50 people happy," and threw 50 1-dollar bills out the door. Quayle, not to be outdone, threw three 100-dollar bills out and said, "That will make three people happy." Bush then said, "I'm going to make 17 million people happy," and threw Quayle out the door.

•

When it was learned that President Bush was A-OK, Quayle had to cancel the decorator for the White House!

Recent polls show that 19% of Americans think that Dan Quayle is smart enough to be President!
When the results of the polls were reported to the VP, he replied "Gee, that's great—more than half!!!"

•

The American people have finally found out why Bush chose Quayle for his Vice-President.
Dan is a perfect tissue match for the President in the event a quick heart transplant is needed.

•

Vice-President Quayle had a problem understanding a program on emergency treatment for heart attacks.
He thought "fibrillating" meant "lying."

•

Later, Bush sent Quayle on another mission—to Central America. Quayle decided that he would book his own flight to Kansas.

By Dana Summers. Copyright 1991, Washington Post Writers Group. Reprinted with permission.

If you think Danny was shook up, how about the rest of the country?
Americans were terrified until they heard that George was okay.

●

If the President's heart fails, the VP is required to be the first in line to provide a transplant organ.

That was Quayle's idea . . . He said, "well, my heart hasn't been in this job to begin with."

●

What made "shock treatment" unnecessary was the thought that Danny would be in charge! A greater "shock" isn't known to medical science!

●

There's a tasty sushi dish called Flying Fish Roe. On top of the fish eggs, they put the yolk of a quail's egg.

George Bush sent Dan Quayle on a mission to Latin America to find out what the people there thought of the President. Quayle spent the next two weeks brushing up on his high school Latin.

•

Quayle has quite a reputation: He said he was looking forward to getting in the Ovum Office.

•

When Dan Quayle heard about Bush's health problem, he went to dial 911. Unfortunately, he couldn't find eleven on the phone.

•

Washington didn't have a college degree, Franklin didn't have a college degree, Jefferson didn't have a college degree, Lincoln didn't have a college degree. Quayle has a college degree.
That's why he's the butt of so many jokes.

If Dan Quayle had worked for Armand Hammer, what would have happened if he had been asked what he wanted to drink? Dan Quayle would probably answer, "Soda, please, the one with the boss's name on it."

•

Here's what Quayle is reported to have said while receiving an honorary degree from a university in Hawaii: "These are islands. They are here. They always have been here, and they always will be." He must have been awarded a Doctor of the Obvious.

•

There's one way Ted Kennedy could become President—if Dan Quayle gets the Republican presidential nomination in 1996

•

How does Quayle order his ice cream?
"I'll take a cone with a dip."

How was Bush kept alive during his hospital stay? If you could overhear two doctors who were on duty you would know:

DOCTOR 1: After some of the treatments didn't work, we suggested that a quick jolt to the heart would correct his heartbeat.

DOCTOR 2: Then we told him that Quayle would act as stand-in President.

•

When George Bush entered the hospital, all of America suffered an irregular heartbeat.

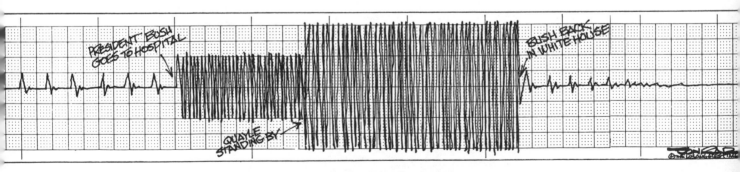

THE HEARTBEAT OF AMERICA

By Paul Conrad. Copyright 1991, Los Angeles Times. Reprinted with permission.

Quayle recently bought a car in Mexico that had four on the floor:
Three illegal aliens and an immigration officer.

•

There was a segment on one of the network news shows about the Dan Quayle Museum. One of the displays is Danny's law degree, which was gnawed upon by his dog.
Now Quayle can honestly say, "My dog ate my degree!"

•

Vice-President Quayle: The OxyMoron of all time . . . in more ways than one.

ON THE ROAD WITH DANFORTH QUAYLE

By Paul Szep. Copyright 1990. Reprinted by permission: The Boston Globe

THIS IS
REALLY.TRUE
(PROBABLY)

Quayle firsts:
First Vice-President to serve as grand marshal for the Indianapolis 500 parade,
First Vice-President to win the Millard Fillmore Medal of Mediocrity, 1990
First Vice-President to be inducted into the Little League Hall of Excellence.

●

Quayle signed an autographed picture to an Indianapolis tailor "To my favorite Taylor."

●

Could Dan really be Clark Kent? If so, why doesn't he fix the ozone holes?

●

Sen. Alan Simpson, recounting how George Bush advised Dan Quayle on how to deal with Quayle jokes:
"You would rather die than live without me!"

What's scarier than Saddam Hussein building a house next door to you? Having Dan Quayle as President, according to a Fall 1990 NBC/*Journal* poll, which found 69% of the people were uncomfortable with the idea of Quayle as President.

•

Even though he was recovering from a double fracture of his right arm, Prince Charles attended the coronation of Japan's Emperor Akihito. All was well until he met up with our Danny boy, whose midwestern enthusiasm at meeting royalty made him pump the prince's hand a little too vigorously. "I was fine until I shook hands with Dan Quayle," said the prince. His recovery set back immeasurably, the bonny prince returned to England where he soon received a note of apology from Dan and a Foam Flex-A-Grip to cushion the royal hand.

•

The Secret Service detail that accompanies Vice-President Dan Quayle and his family on their vacations have come up with a nickname for them: The Griswolds.

After the Vice-President blamed him for causing a recession, Senator George Mitchell responded on NBC's "Meet the Press," "No, I think that's a silly comment." He added: "I get criticized every day by virtue of my position. Some I take seriously, some I don't take seriously. And right at the top of the list of people that I don't take seriously is Dan Quayle." Why should we?

•

Newspaper headline August 12, 1991:
QUAYLE SPEECH SAYS THERE ARE TOO MANY LAWYERS IN US
Newspaper headline August 13, 1991:
QUAYLE RETRACTS REMARKS AFTER REALIZING HE GRADUATED FROM LAW SCHOOL

•

Marilyn Quayle reported that things are looking better for Dan press-wise. "How do you know that?" the Vice-President asked his wife. She replied that while he's given plenty of speeches in the past weeks, she hasn't read a single word about him.

When Marilyn Quayle toured the Charleston area disaster field office she discovered that the two telephone lines they had been able to set up in the office were being overloaded with calls. In the first hour period, more than 300 calls had not been received. "That could have been your husband trying to call you," one official noted.
"I doubt it," she said.

•

Dan Quayle is head of the President's Council on Economic Competitiveness. That explains the recession.

•

Quayle is in favor of a manned mission to Mars: Quayle says that Mars has about the same orbit earth does. "We know that there are canals there and that means there is water there. If there is water,
then there is oxygen, and that means we can breathe there. . . ."

Mars may be the only place Quayle stands a chance of ever being elected President.

In a speech to the World Affairs Council in Philadelphia, Quayle opened a review of his recent trip to Asia with an account of the President's instructions to him before he left: "President Bush called me in," Quayle recalled, smiling, "and he said, 'Our relations with the Pacific Rim nations are very important to the United States.' " Pause.
" 'But I'm going to let you go anyway.' "

•

When he was elected to the Senate in 1980, Quayle told political scientist Richard Fenno, "I know one committee I don't want—Judiciary. They are going to be dealing with all those issues like abortion, busing, voting rights, prayer. I'm not interested in those issues and I want to stay as far away from them as I can."

•

Quayle had this to say about the proposal to put a cap on the number of terms a member of Congress can serve. Quayle said he supports the notion "to limit the terms of members of Congress, especially members of the House and members of the Senate."

During a photo session on the White House lawn, Quayle was giving autographs. A visitor handed Quayle a piece of paper, and without a pen or pencil, the Vice-President made the motions of a signature and handed the blank paper back, moving on. One reporter on the scene quipped that Quayle "must have been using one of those new Stealth pens the Pentagon is working on."

•

Who pays? Not the Quayles. They never opt to make a $1 contribution to the presidential campaign fund when they file their annual taxes.

•

Even the Secret Service seems to take Quayle not-so-seriously. His code name is Scorecard, a reference to his love for golf.

•

Newspaper Headline On Quayle:
HE'S PRETTY, BUT CAN HE TYPE?

Remarking on US strategy in the Persian Gulf, Quayle said, "We are ready for any unforeseen event that may or may not occur."

●

Perquisites of the job: When he was offered a honorary membership in the "Gilligan's Island" Fan Club, the Vice-President turned it down, saying "ethical restraints" prevented his accepting the gift. Still, that didn't stop him from receiving $23,000 in gifts in 1989—including ten pairs of No Excuses blue jeans, two hunting knives worth $2,750, and golfing equipment valued at $2,000. He earns $160,000 a year as Vice-President—plus a generous pension. Quayle supporters donated over $340,000 (tax deductible) for improvements to the Vice-President's residence. This is to supplement the $200,000 for home improvement appropriated by Congress to complement the $378,000 they had previously supplied.

●

Dan gets kind of tired of Washington high life—the fancy
$1,000-a-plate dinners, White House receptions, and dinners
at home with the family chef—so what does he do when he
gets away from Washington? He scarfs down burgers from
Denny's and hot fudge sundaes from Dairy Queen, in addition
to other sweet treats from local groceries and bakeries.
His soft spot for the DQ ice cream is perhaps
related to the fact that the dairy chain and the Vice-President
share the same initials. However, DQ is also a Venezuelan rum,
and an affinity for that could explain a lot of things.

By Rob Rogers. Copyright 1990. Reprinted by permission: UFS, Inc.

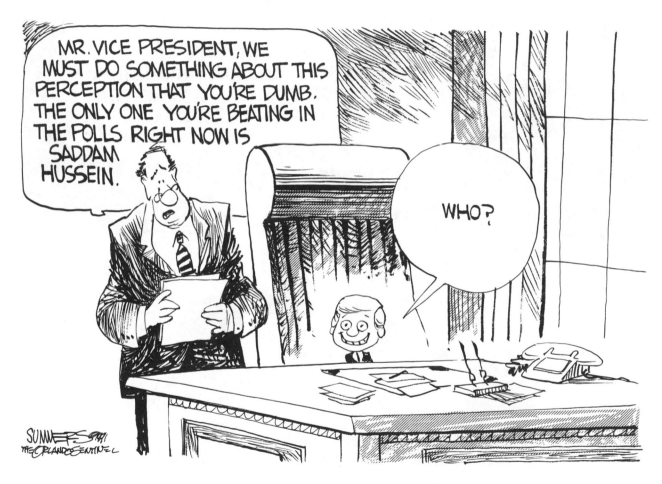

By Dana Summers. Copyright 1991, Washington Post Writers Group. Reprinted with permission.

DID HE REALLY SAY THAT???

Dan's view of Sununu's departure from the White House:
"This isn't a man who is leaving with his head between
his legs."

•

It's tough to be the Vice-President and stuff. "There hasn't been
a Vice-President in history that hasn't been subjected to
ridicule, criticism, and things like that."

•

How can we resist him? "My friends, no matter how rough the
road may be, we can and will, never, never surrender to
what is right."

•

*Nobody's laughing except you, Dan—no wonder your popularity is
so low.* When traffic outside Boston was stopped to clear a
lane for the vice-presidential motorcade, Quayle buzzed
a radio call-in show from his limousine, reporting,
"My lane's clear!"

"I just don't think we ought to look for radical changes in our defense spending posture. The dividend of peace is peace. We've invested in national security, and we got peace," said Quayle to explain the absence of any peace dividend.

•

Quayle called the US victory in the Persian Gulf "a stirring victory for the forces of aggression against lawlessness."

When reporters pointed out what he said, Quayle retracted the statement, saying he meant victory *against* aggression and lawlessness. "I know you find it hard to believe that I misspoke. I appreciate you pointing that out to me so I can clarify that before anyone has the audacity to write down that Dan Quayle somehow misspoke. The American people would not want to know of any misquotes that Dan Quayle may or may not make."

•

Shortly before the budget to build a manned space station was slashed, he said, "Our space program should always go full throttle up."

Foot in Mouth Award: "Need any help?" Quayle asked assembled auto workers in Southgate, Michigan, just two weeks before General Motors announced it would lay off 74,000 people and close 21 plants.

●

In an attempt to defend a beleaguered NASA, Quayle said, "Take it from a guy who knows a lot about unwarranted criticism . . . Once they pile it on, they just don't know when to stop."

●

"Sometimes cameras and television are good to people, and sometimes they aren't. I don't know if it's the way you say it or how you look."

●

"Religion is everything to me. We try to practice what God has communicated to us . . . Religion is life and life after life."

When asked about the future of weapons spending in view of the lessons of the Gulf War, Quayle replied, "This idea of just dropping bombs for the sake of dropping bombs has an impact from a psychological point of view, but from a military-effectiveness point of view, I would certainly question it."

•

We still don't understand why we pay more in taxes. "Let me tell you that the American people know this: that this President doesn't want to raise taxes . . . But the policy now to get a budget reduction package through is: come to the table, no preconditions and let's talk."

•

Does he know the difference between 30 and 80? Although the Rand Corporation's Institute for Civil Justice estimated the "total annual expenditure nationwide for tort lawsuits terminated in 1985 was 29 to $36 billion" Quayle insisted, "One current estimate of the total costs of [product liability] suits is $80 billion per year—a sum larger than the combined profits of the nation's 100 largest corporations."

There is hope. "I just don't believe in the basic concept that someone should make their whole career in public service," said Quayle, regarding his proposed 12-year term limitations for congressional members.

•

"I didn't live in this century," Quayle declared, trying to explain a blooper about the Holocaust.

•

"No one likes ridicule—especially the proud person that I am. I'm very proud of what I've accomplished. When people don't feel the same way I do, obviously I wish they would."

•

Absolutely true
Said Quayle, "One learns every day. Experience is a great teacher. By experience you learn. But as I enter office, I'm prepared now. Obviously, I will be more prepared as time goes on. I will know more about the office of the presidency."

Noting that teachers need fewer material trappings than mere mortals like insurance underwriters, autoworkers, and Vice-Presidents, Quayle pointed out: "Teachers are the only profession that teach our children. It's a unique profession, and by golly, I hope that when they go into the teaching field that they do have that zeal and they do have that mission and they do believe in teaching our kids and they're not getting into this just as a job or a way to put food on the table."

•

Never one to let facts get in the way, Quayle blithely stated: "From an historical basis, Middle East conflicts do not last a long time."

•

He pronounced Latin American hero Simon Bolívar as *Seaman Believer.*

•

Another: "I stand by all the misstatements that I've made."

Arguing the case for respect for Americans in the Middle East, Dan said, "Never have we been invited into a country like we were into Saudi Arabia. You don't invite someone into your country if you don't have respect."

•

If you think he's out of touch with the feelings of regular Americans, listen to what he had to say about the plight of Iraqis after the Gulf War: "We do not have any plan that's going to go in there and impose a government for the people of Iraq; this is their problem."

•

Here's something really interesting Dan said: "Hawaii has always been a very pivotal role in the Pacific. It is a part of the United States that is an island that is right here."

•

Quayle called the proposed limit on congressional terms, "an idea whose time was about to arrive."

When Bush was in the hospital with heart problems, Dan had this to say: "The first question I had was, 'Was it serious?' And at no time during the three days was it ever stated to me that it was serious. At no time was there any sense of urgency. It was extraordinarily normal, considering the circumstances."

•

"While I have not apologized for my National Guard Service, and never will, I recognize that the members of my generation who served in Vietnam made a sacrifice that was far, far greater than mine."

•

Said Quayle: "What a waste it is to lose one's mind, or not to have a mind." He added, "How true that is."

•

Quayle Quote on the concept of a manned mission to Mars: It's "time for the human race to enter the solar system."

Even though he hardly figures in foreign policy, Quayle noted he was on top of issues in the Middle East during the fall 1990 Gulf Crisis because he met with Bush daily. "Every day that I'm in Washington we meet for an hour and a half to two hours. I'm in continuous contact with him and the situation room when we're apart."

•

More trouble with numbers. "One word sums up probably the responsibility of any Vice-President, and that one word is 'to be prepared.'" Isn't that the Boy Scout motto, anyway?

•

Quayle Quote: "People that are really very weird can get into sensitive positions and have a tremendous impact on history."

•

After his inauguration, Quayle said, "They asked me to go in front of the Reagans. I'm not used to going in front of President Reagan, so we went out behind the Bushes."

No wonder he visits Latin America so often! "Many of these leaders are younger than I am. It's the only area of the world where Dan Quayle is considered an elder statesman," said Quayle.

●

Don't forget, "If we don't succeed, we run the risk of failure."

●

This is a statement in and of itself. "Japan is an important ally of ours. Japan and the United States of the western industrialized capacity, sixty percent of the GNP, two countries.
That's a statement in and of itself."

●

Late fan of the UN: "I was exceedingly skeptical of the United Nations. But after seeing how President Bush worked the UN, I have altered my viewpoint. Before, my tendency was to dismiss it as a soapbox. I don't view it that way anymore."

Quayle Quote: "We are the most powerful planet on earth."

•

Stand by your Dan. Says Marilyn Quayle: "It would be a pretty sorry world if people weren't allowed to slip up and be human. You don't want anyone who is rotely perfect running this country."

By Paul Conrad. Copyright 1988, Los Angeles Times. Reprinted with permission.

DAN ON THE CAMPAIGN TRAIL

When the Vice-President announced he would be a "pit bull" during the 1992 campaign, Bill Clinton, a Democratic candidate for the presidency, reacted, "My, that's got every fire hydrant in America worried."

•

"Vote for Dan Quayle—Definitely Not the Dumbest Guy in the Deke House." Calvin Trillin, 1988 in *The Nation*.

•

What was George Bush's campaign slogan?
BUSH AND BUSH LITE

•

Dan Quayle lets George Bush look charismatic.

•

Dan Quayle is the man who makes everyone feel smarter.

But as the election comes up, you know what they'll be calling Dan? George Bush's golfing handicap.

•

The ultimate Dan Quayle joke has to be: DAN QUAYLE, VICE-PRESIDENT.

•

What's the makeup of the Republican ticket for the White House? A Yankee and a Dodger.

•

It's the mid-1990's. Quayle's new Vice-President says, "Dan you've just been elected President. What do you want to do first?"
Quayle: "Go to Disneyland!"

By Mike Luckovich. Copyright 1989. Reprinted by permission: Mike Luckovich and Creators Syndicate.

By Steve Kelley. Copyright 1988. Reprinted with permission: Copeley News Service.

ON·THE·HOME·FRONT

What's the favorite chicken dish at the Vice-President's table?
Fried right wings.

•

Did you hear how Dan met his wife, Marilyn? She caught him peeking at her paper during the bar exam.

•

You can be fairly certain that you'll never see "The Dan Quayle Selective Service Office."

•

What did Marilyn say to Dan on their wedding night?
"You're no Jack Kennedy."

•

When Marilyn Quayle is in a sexy mood, she leans over and blows in her husband's ear. "Thanks for the refill," Dan replies.

•

"I haven't read it [Doonesbury] in five years. It hasn't been funny in five years," says number-one Dan supporter, Marilyn. Doonesbury cartoonist Gary Trudeau's portrayal of Quayle is merciless, and hey, it was about five years ago that Dan Quayle was thrust into the national spotlight.

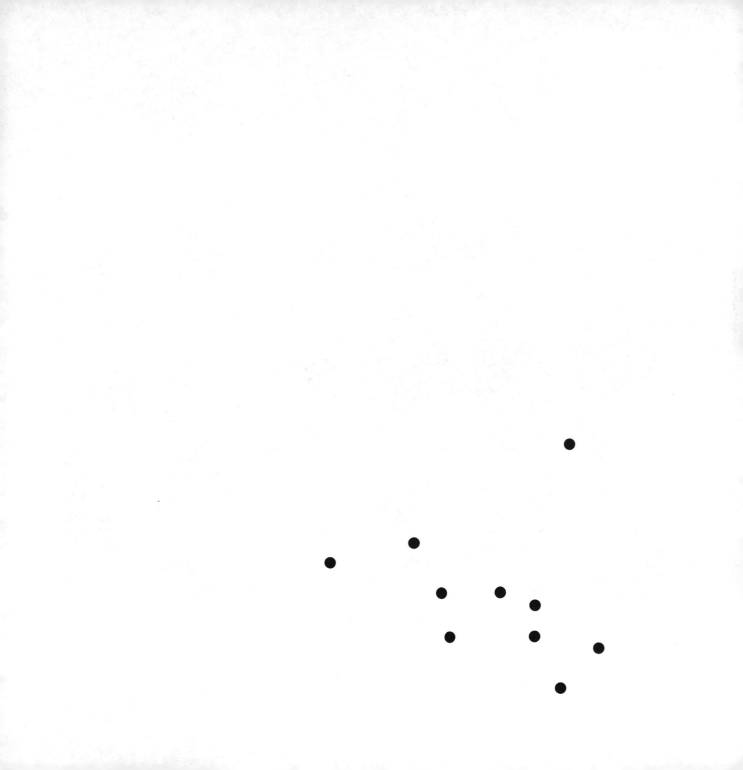

By Doug Marlette. Copyright 1989. Reprinted by permission: Doug Marlette and Creators Syndicate.

DAN-INSPIRED ART

STAND BY YOUR DAN

Capitol Steps parody of "Stand by Your Man"

BUSH
It's hard to run the Oval Office
Everyone ignores what I propose
Nor I'll detail why
I chose that Quayle guy I chose
One day I saw the "Wheel of Fortune"
Get me that Sajak guy, I said
But then his mother
Sent his twin brother
I should have bought a vowel instead

Stand by your Dan
I'll work him till he's dizzy
Just like I keep kids busy
Inside my clan
My handyman
While overseas I'm going
That White House lawn needs mowing, Dan

DAN'S DAD
Sometimes it's hard to be Dan's father
I know my Danny's grades were bad
This needy student
Was really prudent
He picked the perfect Mom and Dad

Stand in for Dan
I always prop his tush up
That's why I called George Bush up
To pick my Dan
I have a plan
So I got Dan and Bush in
There's one more place I'm pushin' Dan
The Vatican!

TALK LIKE A DAN

Capitol Steps parody of "Walk Like a Man"

INTRO   Ladies and gentlemen, we have a special treat for you
tonight. It seems that the Vice-President of the
United States, the Honorable J. Danforth
Quayle, is going to tell us everything that's on
his mind.

CHORUS   Ooh-ooh-ooh, oops, oops, (etc.)

DAN   When George Bush first asked me to be Vice-
President, he said, "Dan, don't get any ideas."
No problem.

(sung)   My name's Danny Quayle
I didn't go to Yale
Got C's and D's at Indiana U.
What I'll confess is
The key to my success is
You talk like me, and you'll be famous too

BASS   If you just . . .

ALL   Talk like a Dan, much as you can
Talk like a Dan, my son

That's how to plan to be a famous man
And Georgie will be your fan

DAN
(spoken)

I can't wait to see the day when America
can land a man on the sun. Well, I guess it
would be kind
of hot. Maybe we should do it at night.

(sung)

I say happy campers
My staff puts on the dampers
They stand by my misstatements that they traced
My scripts all are no-gos
Call Pango Pongo Pongo
A mindless mind no one would mind to waste.

BASS

Because you . . .

ALL

Talk like a Dan, much as you can, ooh (etc.)

DAN
(spoken)

When I was just a newborn, and the doctor cut
my imbecilical cord, I never dreamed that I
would head up a commission that would run the
whole NASA space program. Because when I was
young people always said to me, "Dan . . .
you're no rocket scientist."

BASS

Because you . . .

ALL

Talk like a Dan, much as you can
Talk like a Dan, my son

DAN	Just take a look, I'm working on a book
CHORUS	Next year we'll see if Dan can
DAN	Color another one

The Capitol Steps:
Musical political satire without party loyalty
You can purchase Capitol Steps records, tapes, and CDs
1-800-733-STEP
or
Capitol Steps Productions
1505 King St.
Alexandria, VA 22314

115
•
DAN-INSPIRED
ART

The Love Song of J. Danforth Quaylefrock

by Tim Grana
First appeared in the Winter/Spring 1991 issue of *The Quayle Quarterly*

Let's tee off then, you and me
When the morning is spread out along the greens
Like a liberal thunderstruck by my pronouncements;
Let's drive balls like certain half-perverted creeps,
The shutterbugging peeps
Of Swaggart's nights in one-night hotel rooms
With high speed Kodachrome and Nikon zooms:
Creeps that wallow like ridiculous elephants
Or insipid sycophants
To strand you in a devastating muddle . . .
Oh, do not ask "where George is."
Let us go and raise some gorges.

In the House the lawmen kink and warp
Balking at Robert Mapplethorpe

The yellow streak that runs its course upon my spinal chord.
The yellow spot that stains my belly with its rhinal hoard
Licked its tongue into the backside of the mighty,
Lingered upon the fools that call the shots,
Let call upon its dad the snoot that comes from privilege

Slipped in a banknote, did a little graft
And seeing that it was a tough quagmire fight
Joined the National Guard, and dodged the draft.

And indeed there will be slime
From the yellow streak that runs along my back
Keeping my butt out of the Army Corps;
There will be slime, there will be slime
To discharge some mace to greet the faces that you beat;
There will be slime for items and reviews
And slime from all the twists and turns of tongues
That slip and drop a whopper on the news;
Slime from you and slime from me,
And slime yet from a hundred fusions and confusions
Before the swinging of a club at tee.

In the House the lawmen kink and warp
Balking at Robert Mapplethorpe
And indeed there will be *Time*
To ponder, "Am I dull?" and, "Am I dull?"
Time to whitewash and the voters gull,
With the blank space in the middle of my skull—
(They will say: "How can George control this spin?")
My garbled speech, my syntax tangled badly state it's in,
My logic medieval, full of dancing angels on a pin—
(They will say: "But how his brain is wafer thin!")
Am I dull

Despite the long rehearse?
Just a minute, here is *Time*
With illusions and contusions no spin doctor can reverse!

For I have blown them all already, blown them all—
Have blown the photos, soundbytes, interviews,
I have measured out my life with autocues;
I know the voices sighing with a lying stall
Beneath the fallout from some Bush mischance
      Is that how I'll advance?

And I have known the jibes already, known them all—
The jibes that jinx you in such ridiculing spoofs,
And when I am ridiculed, drawling like an oaf,
When I am punned and sniveling in the Mall,
Then how should I take oath
To spit out all the sound-bytes of my bloops and goofs?
      And how should I advance?

And I have known the arms already, known them all—
Arms that are fissionable and mean and low
(But in photos, aimed at my elbow!)
Is it questions from the press
That cause me such distress?
Arms that slip across the border, and stop the Contra's fall.
      And should I then advance?
      And how should I take oath?

Shall I say, I have cast a gaze at launching pads
And craved the glow that halos round the heads
Of astronauts in space suits, hanging out at NASA?

I should have been a doll with throbbing parts
Flashing among the peaks of high Andes.

And the people, the voters, dupe so easily!
Conned by campaigners
Beguiled . . . bored . . . or they're abstainers
Stretched on the rack, here by the GOP.
Should I, after pleas and aches and vices,
Have the nerve to make a speech on the Gulf Crisis?
But though I've been coached and prompted, coached
    and primed,
Though I have seen my prose (by Galbraith gored) reduced
    to scarce a tatter,
I am no statesman—for here's no grey matter;
I have seen the grandees of my party truckle,
And I have seen the infernal Pollster take my pulse,
    and chuckle,
and in short, I was begrimed.

And would I still be sworn in, in a year,
After the gaffes, the malaprops, the tease,
Among the columnists, among some talk of bribes and sleaze,
Could it have been my style

To have wandered off the matter by a mile,
To have teased constituents inside a sphere
To roll them toward some devastating muddle
To say: "I am Danforth come to this land,
Looks like campers, here, happy campers here"—
If one, dropping a ballot from her hand,
    Should say: "Now that's what I call the nadir.
    This guy's a jerk, I fear."

And could I still be sworn in, in a year,
Could I have been servile
After the jet sets and the blowhards and the crinkled cheats
After the bungles, after the slipups, after the deals that
fail to lose their smells—
And this, and so much else?—
It is impossible to mean just what I say!
But as if a Barbara Walters dished the dirt in headlines
  on "Today":
Would it have been hostile
If one, casting a ballot or tossing off a beer,
And turning toward the camera, should moan:
    "This guy's a jerk, I fear.
    Now that's what I call the nadir."

No! I'm no Kennedy, nor could ever be
Am an appalling bore, one that will do
To raise a titter, like a Spiro Agnew

Surprise the Chief; no doubt, a sleazy klutz
Presidential, silly as a goose
Pathetic, bumptious, and preposterous
Full of bull piddle, but a bit obtuse;
At times, indeed, almost disastrous
Almost, at times, a putz.

I blow dope . . . I blow dope . . .
I shall call the US a "beakon" of hope.

Shall I put more hair spray on? Do I dare to meet the press?
I shall be a rabble-rouser, and make a mighty mess.
I have left the experts weeping, more or less.

I do not think that they will vote for me.

I have seen them writing for *The New York Times*
Mocking the wife's hair of Dippity-Do
Though I wrap myself in red, white, and blue.

I've been foisted on the chamber of the Hill
Where call girls hired by Tower ground and bumped
Till George's ratings plummet, and I'm dumped.

Subscriptions to The Quayle Quarterly are $14.95.
Contact The Quayle Quarterly,
P.O. Box 8593, Brewster Station,
Bridgeport, CT 06605.

By Paul Conrad. Copyright 1991, Los Angeles Times. Reprinted with permission.

DAN'S OWN JOKES

Quayle actually created laughter in Raleigh, North Carolina, when a reporter said she would ask about "the dreaded T-word: taxes." "Oh," he said, appearing relieved, "I thought you were going to say textiles."

•

Quayle's 1990 trip to Chile had its rough spots. Two days before he arrived, ten bombs exploded near the US Consulate in Santiago. When he got there, he was greeted by Pinochet supporters who beat and kicked his car while shouting obscenities. "I've had worse crowds," responded Quayle when he spoke of the experience.

•

The problem with Democrats, Quayle says, is they could lead the country "past backwardness."

•

On Nolan Ryan: "I love it when I hear the media describe someone 44 years of age as mature and well seasoned."

Sure the press caught him when he purchased the aroused Chilean doll, but Dan says they missed a great opportunity when on a trip to England he "showed that doll to Margaret Thatcher."

•

"[Bush] has said a number of times, 'I've got a whole drawer full of press clippings from when I was Vice-President. If you ever feel down, help yourself.' And I said, 'No, Mr. President, that's OK. I read them, too.'"

•

Quayle on former Secretary of State James A. Baker III, and 1988 campaign manager:
"I owe him so much," he said. "During the campaign he took me under his wing. And kept me there." He said Baker advised before his vice-presidential campaign debate with Lloyd Bentson, "Wait for a strategic moment, then compare yourself to John Kennedy."

•

About his relationship with the President: "I think the President truly appreciates my insights," he said. "Just the other day he was telling the Cabinet, 'If there's one thing I won't tolerate, it's yes men. Isn't that right, Dan?' "

•

On the jokes about his youth and lack of experience: "What really burned me up were all the stories about my so-called handlers. I finally got so mad I went right to the top. I said, 'Marilyn, you've got to do something about this.' "

•

On the Dukakis campaign: "Want to hear a sad story about the Dukakis campaign?" Quayle asked. "The governor of Massachusetts, he lost his top naval adviser last week. His rubber duck drowned in his bathtub."

•

AMEN.

ABOUT THE AUTHORS

BILL ADLER is a literary agent, book packager, and president of Bill Adler Books, Inc. He is the author of dozens of books, and the creator of numerous best-sellers including *Who Killed the Robbins Family?* He and his wife live in New York City.

BILL ADLER, JR., is a literary agent, book packager, and president of Adler & Robin Books, Inc. He is the author of a dozen books including the much-acclaimed *Outwitting Squirrels*. He lives with his wife and daughter in Washington, DC.